Your Mission on Earth

D1710877

by Christine Zuchora-Walske
illustrated by Scott Burroughs

Content Consultant
Diane M. Bollen, Research Scientist,
Cornell University

magic
wagon

visit us at www.abdopublishing.com

Published by Magic Wagon, a division of the ABDO Group, 8000 West 78th Street, Edina, Minnesota, 55439. Copyright © 2012 by Abdo Consulting Group, Inc. International copyrights reserved in all countries. All rights reserved. No part of this book may be reproduced in any form without written permission from the publisher.

Looking Glass Library™ is a trademark and logo of Magic Wagon.

Printed in the United States of America, North Mankato, Minnesota.
052011
092011
 THIS BOOK CONTAINS AT LEAST 10% RECYCLED MATERIALS.

Text by Christine Zuchora-Walske
Illustrations by Scott Burroughs
Edited by Holly Saari
Series design and cover production by Becky Daum
Interior production by Christa Schneider

Library of Congress Cataloging-in-Publication Data
Zuchora-Walske, Christine.
  Your mission on Earth / by Christine Zuchora-Walske ; illustrated by Scott Burroughs.
     p. cm. — (The planets)
  Includes bibliographical references and index.
  ISBN 978-1-61641-677-5 (alk. paper)
  1. Earth—Juvenile literature. I. Burroughs, Scott, ill. II. Title.
  QB631.4.Z83 2012
  525—dc22
                                    2011006774

Table of Contents

Going into Space

We're so lucky we live on Earth! It has everything we need to survive. And it's beautiful. Blue skies and green grass and trees surround us.

Barely anybody gets to leave Earth. We are kept here because of Earth's gravity. But you are lucky. You have a spacecraft ready to jet you into outer space. Blast off!

Solar System

In your spacecraft, you find a map of our solar system. Your map shows eight planets orbiting the sun. The sun is our solar system's star. Earth is the third planet from the sun. The sun is about 93 million miles (150 million km) away from our planet.

View from Space

Hundreds of miles up, your spacecraft starts orbiting Earth. You look out the window.

Earth is lovely! You see that most of Earth is covered in blue water. You look at the white swirls of clouds. You spot the green land.

Oceans cover about 70 percent of Earth's surface.

Water

Earth's water is important. All living things need water. Most of Earth's water is liquid. This is because of Earth's distance from the sun. If Earth were closer to the sun, the water would boil away into the air. If Earth were farther from the sun, the water would freeze into ice.

Interior

Earth is made of rock and metal. The shell of rock and soil around Earth is called the crust. A layer of mostly hot, solid rock called the mantle lies below. Under that it gets really hot. This outer core is molten iron. Earth's inner core is solid iron.

Earth's crust is cracked. The pieces move. When they spread apart or bump together, volcanoes erupt or earthquakes tremble. Over millions of years, mountains form.

Atmosphere

You see Earth's atmosphere from space. It looks like a light blue outline around the planet.

Our air is mostly nitrogen and oxygen. Our air also contains tiny amounts of other gases, like carbon dioxide. These gases hold the sun's heat near Earth's surface so it's warm enough for us to live.

Life on Earth

Earth is very special. As far as we know, it's the only planet with intelligent life. How long has life existed on Earth?

You do some research. Many scientists believe the smallest life-forms came into being about 3.5 billion years ago. That was way before dinosaurs existed! Over those billions of years, life became more and more complex—like you!

Days and Years

As your spacecraft orbits Earth, you zoom toward and away from the sun. You see the sun every one-and-a-half hours. It's kind of like a sunrise in space. But you know that on Earth, the time between sunrises is 24 hours. That equals one day.

Earth spins like a top. As it spins toward the sun, the sun appears to rise. As Earth spins away from the sun, the sun appears to set. The time from sunrise to sunrise is one day.

While Earth spins, it also orbits the sun. The time it takes a planet to orbit the sun is one year. One year on Earth is about 365 days.

On one half of Earth, it is day. That's the side facing the sun. On the other half, it is night. That is the part facing away from the sun.

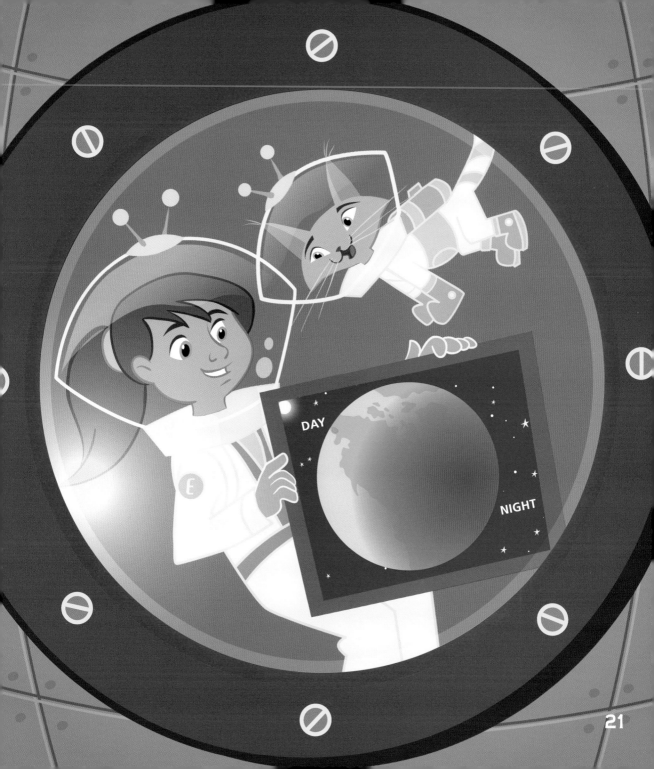

Seasons

Earth spins at a tilt. As Earth moves in its orbit, different parts of the planet are tilted toward the sun. This is why Earth has seasons. The part that is tilted toward the sun has summer. The part that is tilted away from the sun has winter.

Space Junk

You notice that you've got company up here. Thousands of human-made objects orbit Earth. The bigger ones are spacecrafts or old satellites. The smaller ones are junk left behind by spacecrafts. This includes paint flakes and space gear.

Scientists work aboard some of the spacecrafts, like the International Space Station. Most of the crafts are satellites with no passengers. Satellites are used so people on Earth can make cell phone calls and watch shows on television.

Moon

The biggest object orbiting Earth is the moon. It's about one-fourth as wide as Earth. It orbits about 238,855 miles (384,400 km) away. You head toward the moon. It takes you a few hours to get there.

As you near the moon, you see mountains, rocky plains, and many craters. You carefully land your craft where it is flat.

The moon is made of solid rock. You step onto the rocks and powdery dust on its surface. You see your cat meowing, but you can't hear her. You remember reading that there is no air in space. Because of that, there is no sound, either. You shout a hello back to Earth to test this. You can't hear yourself!

You're excited to get back to Earth. There, all your friends and family can hear you shout hello to them!

How Do Scientists Know So Much about Earth?

It is easy to study Earth because we live here. For hundreds of years, though, people believed Earth was flat. They thought the sky was a solid dome overhead, with stars hanging like lanterns. They also believed the sun, moon, stars, and other planets orbited Earth. Thousands of years ago, Greek scientists figured out that Earth is round. But most of them still believed that Earth was the center of the universe.

In the early 1500s, scientist Nicolaus Copernicus stated Earth and other planets orbit the sun. Scientists argued about this for many years. In the late 1600s, scientist Isaac Newton figured out how gravity works. This idea helped convince the world that Copernicus was right. Earth is just one of many planets orbiting one of many stars in a huge universe.

During the 1600s, scientific thought and research exploded. Since then, all the sciences—biology, chemistry, math, astronomy, physics, geology, engineering, and dozens more—have improved greatly. These sciences help us learn about our planet's land, water, and air. In 1957, scientists launched the *Sputnik* satellites. This began the space age, a new era of studying Earth from space.

Earth Facts

Position: Third planet from sun

Distance from sun: 93 million miles (150 million km)

Diameter (distance through the planet's middle): 7,926 miles (12,756 km)

Length of orbit (year): Approximately 365 days

Length of rotation (day): Approximately 24 hours

Number of moons: 1

Words to Know

atmosphere—the layer of gases surrounding a planet.

core—the center of a planet.

crater—a dip in the ground shaped like a large bowl.

gas—a substance that spreads out to fit what it is in, like air in a tire.

gravity—the force that pulls a smaller object toward a larger object.

mantle—the part of a planet between the crust and the core.

orbit—to travel around something, usually in an oval path.

satellite—a natural or human-made object in space that orbits a planet.

solar system—a star and the objects, such as planets, that travel around it.

Learn More

Books

Simon, Seymour. *Our Solar System.* Washington DC: Smithsonian, 2007.

Wells, Robert E. *What's So Special About Planet Earth?* Morton Grove, IL: Albert Whitman, 2009.

Yasuda, Anita. *Explore the Solar System!* White River Junction, VT: Nomad Press, 2009.

Web Sites

To learn more about Earth, visit ABDO Group online at **www.abdopublishing.com**. Web sites about Earth are featured on our Book Links page. These links are routinely monitored and updated to provide the most current information available.

Index